FIGHTER MEET

AIR SHOW COLOUR SCHEMES

C000003978

FIGHTER MEET

AIR SHOW COLOUR SCHEMES

C. J. van Gent

J. K. A. Bontje

Airlife
England

ACKNOWLEDGEMENTS

The 'Colourful eighties' — ten roaring years in military aviation. Well-known aircraft types disappeared and were succeeded by others. Airforces and their squadrons celebrated jubilees; aircraft and airmen both achieved record numbers of flying hours. Altogether enough events to provide the illustrated material for this book.

Of course the writer could not personally witness all these events, taking into consideration that the content of this collection covers occasions throughout the European NATO countries and Canada. The realization of this album was to a high extent possible because of the cordial co-operation of many people and military authorities. Friends, acquaintances and, last but not least, my correspondents 'all over the world' contributed significant material.

Alphabetically, I list their names:

Stenio Bacciocchi (Italy), Humbert Charve (France), Regent Dansereau (Canada), Frank H. Elsinga (The Netherlands), Roberto Farina (Italy), Michel Fournier (France), L. C. Friedrichs (The Netherlands), Richard W. Gennis (Britain), Jan JØrgensen (Denmark), Daniel Loreille (France), Herman J. Sixma (The Netherlands), Ivo Sturzenegger (Switzerland), Dirk Tabak (The Netherlands), Kurt Thomsen (Germany), Ben J. Ullings (The Netherlands), Peter van Weenen (The Netherlands), Jos Wigbold (The Netherlands).

Not least I would like to thank the Public Relations units of the Royal Netherlands and Belgian Air Force HQ. They provided a considerable number of beautiful air-to-air photos. For the RNethA/F this material was made available by the Fotosectie of Soesterberg A/B. Not only the Public Relations department of the Belgian A/F but also Roels Antoine of the VS1/IRP, J. Huybens and Ulrich de Bruyn I wish to thank for their co-operation.

Of the French Armée de l'Air I mention the Groupement Ecole 315 of Cognac A/B.

Special thanks go to Second Lieutenant Barbara L. Masse of DND Office of Information North Bay, Canadian Forces.

Also to be mentioned is Axel Osterman, former demo-pilot of the Vikings of the Bundesmarine. Still an enthusiastic pilot within the Bundesmarine, he nowadays flies the Tornado. His Luftwaffe colleague, Major Gottfried Schwarz, proved to be not only a good pilot but an observant photographer too.

We also express our thanks to those military authorities who made it possible to produce the material included in this book. Last but most certainly not least because they should have been mentioned in the first place, I owe grateful thanks to my friend Jan Bontje who translated the text, and to both our wives (Annemiek and Marijke) — the latter because they have supported us even in difficult periods.

Many names will undoubtedly have been forgotten for reasons easy to understand. It took ten years to gather the material for this book. Material has been presented by many people from many countries, often anonymous and more than once of the same machine. If your name has not been mentioned, be assured that my gratitude is beyond doubt.

Military aircraft are more and more and for many reasons being painted in beautiful outfits. More countries than ever before are likely to follow suit and it may well be that another book along the lines of this one will appear. In order to realize this, I appeal to the reader of this book. If you think that in the future you might contribute to such a book by means of slides or colour-pictures do not hesitate to send me the material via the publisher. In that case do not forget to add an explanation and of course your name and address.

First published in the UK in 1991 by
Airlife Publishing Limited

Printed in Singapore by Kyodo Printing PTE Ltd.

Airlife Publishing Limited

101 Longden Road, Shrewsbury, England

Copyright © C. J. van Gent, 1991

All rights reserved. No part of this book may be reproduced or transmitted in any form or by any means, electronic or mechanical including photocopying, recording or by any information storage and retrieval system, without permission from the Publisher in writing.

INTRODUCTION

Painting military aircraft in eye-catching special colours is not too rare a phenomena. Over the years many airforces have had in common the necessity of presenting themselves to the public. For that purpose, open days with an airshow to finalize the 'circus' were mostly used. Often the display of special demonstration aircraft, solo or as a team, was literally the high point, drawing the attention of the public. To secure this attention the aircraft were occasionally painted in fascinating colours.

This book will concentrate on a quite contemporary aspect of special colours in military aviation. A tendency that above all set the tone of the eighties was the use of special paintings on aircraft to mark some kind of celebration. This could be the jubilee of a squadron or the retirement of a certain type of airplane; the introduction of a new type or even the number of flying hours of a particular machine, its squadron or its pilot.

The story of the international Tiger-meet, which may have led to this trend of distinctive colours, is unique. Started in 1961 it almost happened by chance that the host squadron of the yearly exercise painted one of its planes in "tiger colours". These decorative machines caught and held everyone's attention and it is not difficult to under-

stand that this example was soon and often followed. A separate chapter of this book will focus on this subject.

Although the United States had already coloured her military planes in 'bicentennial schemes' to mark her 200th anniversary in 1976, this period fell before the 'eighties and outside Europe. This epoch therefore plays no role in this book which concentrates on European NATO airforces. Yet pictures of Europe-based USAF aircraft have been included.

In Europe the Luftwaffe set the fashion. Various squadrons spontaneously painted 'their' planes during celebrations. Initially just a tiny ribbon or a coloured tail were used but gradually the kites got more and more lively-coloured. Many airforces followed their steps. Glancing through this book you will notice this ascending and escalating tendency. Though a book like this simply cannot be anything but incomplete it shows a vivid silhouette of this aspect of military aviation in the last decade in Western Europe. Often the depicted planes are a notable piece of art in sometimes exotic but always eye-catching colour schemes.

We hope you will have as much joy in looking at the result now in your hands, as we have had in preparing it!

BELGIUM

Below & Opposite: In June 1984 the 42nd smaldeel[1] at Florennes Airbase commemorated its founding 30 years earlier. Two Mirage 5BRs, BR–04 and BR–22, were painted with a large squadron emblem on the tail.

Overleaf: July 15th 1985 marked the 15th anniversary of the 8th smaldeel at Bierset. Though the party was limited to 'an internal affair' the Mirage 5BA with serial BA–63 was nevertheless painted with a special scheme.

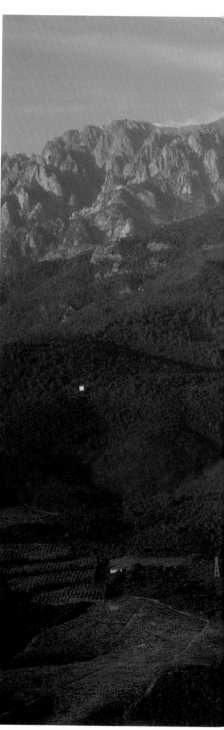

[1] squadron

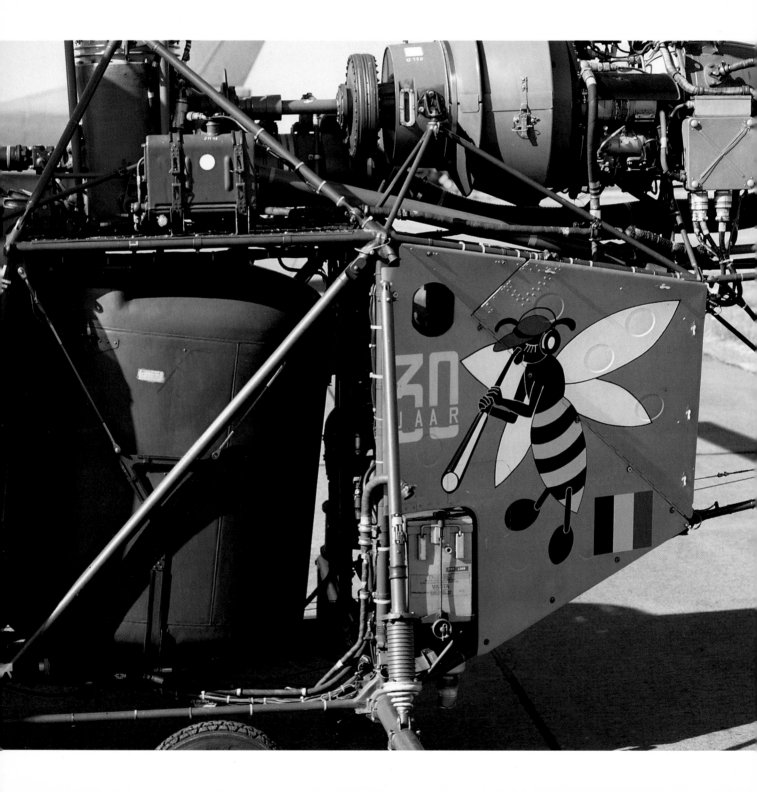

Opposite & Bottom: The 18th smaldeel of the Landmacht[2] on point-duty at Aachen-Merzbruck (GFR) commemorated its 30th anniversary in 1986. The Alouette 2 with serial A-80 was painted with a big insignia on a blue background. Here we see the heli on Koksijde Airbase during the airshow of July 17th 1986.

Below: The OT-ZKH/B-8 was not only the last Sikorsky S-58/HSS-1 operational with the 40th smaldeel, but also the last one in military dress in Europe. On July 19th 1986 it made its final flight from Koksijde. At the same time fell the anniversary of the founding of the 'Heliflight' on April 1st 1961. The whole event was dominated by the commemoration of 25 years of SAR (Search and Rescue).

Below & Opposite: With this F-16A, the FA-18, smaldeel 350 demonstrated the celebration of its 45th anniversary on Beauvechain Airbase on November 12th 1986. One year later this machine, meanwhile named 'vuurzee' (inferno) was displayed at many airshows; here we see it at Brustem on June 27th 1987

Right & Opposite: The 1st smaldeel at Bierset held a seventieth birthday party on May 23rd 1987. One Mirage 5–BA was painted with a large yellow thistle on a black background. Dressed like a 'blackbird' this Mirage visited many a meeting!

Below: On June 27th and 28th 1987 Brustem held an airshow to mark the 40th anniversary of the vliegschool. An Alpha Jet of the 9th Wing bearing serial AT–29 was painted in the national colours. When the festivities were over, the numeral '40' was removed from the tail but for many years this plane went on as a show-piece carrying the national 'tricolour' at many events.

Below & Opposite: One week later, on May 30th 1987, smaldeel 2 also celebrated 70 years. Of course it had to keep up with the 1st smaldeel and therefore Mirage 5–BA with serial BA–43 was painted in a bizarre manner which promptly gave it the name of 'Milky-way'.

Below & Opposite: On May 27th 1988 it was the turn of 349 smaldeel of Beauvechain to recall the fact that 45 years ago this squadron was founded. An F–16A with serial FA–49 was dressed up with an immense squadron emblem, composed of two medieval clubs named 'goedendag' ('morning star') on the back. It became famous as 'Bluebird'.

Below & Opposite: Again a 70th anniversary; this time smaldeel 11 of Brustem on October 7th 1988. This Alpha Jet with serial AT–11 was dressed up in a special 'coat' and was supposed to represent a bat. A little imagination is needed to recognize batplane . . .

Below & Opposite: The Fouga CM–170
Magister celebrates thirty years in active
service. Reason enough for a special dress
during a meeting at Bierset on September
10th 1989 by means of the MT–30 of the 30th
smaldeel. All emblems used through the years
were incorporated in the painting on the nose.

Above & Opposite: On January 26th 1989 at Beauvechain the day was recalled when ten years before the F–16 joined the Belgian Airforce. The first plane to be delivered to the Belgians, the FB–01, was furnished with an attractive tail outfit. All the emblems of each Belgian Airforce F–16 squadron were included.

CANADA

Below & Opposite: To celebrate its 40 years of
existence in 1982, 421 'Red Indian' Squadron at
Baden Söllingen (GFR) painted its CF–104G
104868 in special colours. The aircraft was thus
shown on a number of occasions, as here at
Toul (France). This particular plane was not
unknown, since it showed off its white tail at
the Tactical Air Meet at Wildenrath (GFR).

Below & Opposite: CT–33A 133345 of GTTF (Group Training and Transit Flight) at CFB Söllingen, painted in a spectacular scheme to celebrate its 10,000th flying hour! Here it is displayed during the 30th anniversary show at Söllingen on June 11 1983.

Below: At the same show at Söllingen, 421 'Red Indian' Squadron showed its CF–104G Starfighter 104805 painted in an eye-catching fashion with the squadron colours.

Opposite: 441 'Silver Fox' Squadron at CFB Söllingen wears a 'black and white checkerboard pattern' for its 30th anniversary airshow on June 11 and 12 1983. CF–104G 104880 was changed as if by magic into a 'Checkerbird'.

Below: To commemorate its 25 years of
existence 419 Squadron of CFB Cold Lake
painted this CF–5A 116703 in 'warm' colours.

Opposite: CP–121 Tracker 12195 of 880
Squadron at CFB Summerside, wearing a
bright blue and gold tail to mark the unit's 30th
anniversary in 1987.

THE CF–101B VOODOO IN CANADIAN SERVICE

The CF–101 Voodoo was introduced in the Canadian Armed Forces in the early sixties when four squadrons of the RCAF were equipped with this type.

In 1961 and 1962, 410 'Cougar' and 425 'Alouette' Squadrons of Bagotville, 409 'Night Hawk' Squadron of Comox, and 416 'Lynx' Squadron of Chatham were equipped with 66 Voodoos in total (55 CF–101B and 10 CF–101F). These were all built by McDonnell-Douglas.

Since the summer of 1983 each of the four Voodoo squadrons has been stood down. First 410 Squadron was converted to the CF–18 operational training squadron. Shortly afterwards 409 Squadron ceased using the Voodoo to become the first operational CF–18 Squadron. The remaining 425 and 416 Squadrons also exchanged the Voodoo for the CF–18 and in December 1984 the CAF stopped all operations with the CF–101, except for one aircraft. Before the CAF ended all operations with the CF–101, four Voodoos in special colours made a farewell flight in the summer of 1984.

One aircraft — the black Voodoo 101067 with red markings — has its own story. The CAF received this aircraft at the beginning of the eighties and modified it to an EF–101B for ECM duties. The aircraft was operated by the 414 'Electronic Warfare' Squadron and was well-known as the 'Electric' Voodoo.

When the CAF retired all their Voodoos from operational service this EF–101B still remained in service. As the very last Voodoo it was phased out by the end of 1986. It was the end of a very popular aircraft.

Opposite: CF–101B 101043 of 416 'Lynx' Squadron at Chatham Air Base.

Opposite: The 'Hawk One' was the CF–101B 101057 of 409 'Night Hawk' Squadron at Comox AB.

Below: The beautifully dressed CF–101B 101014 of 425 'Lark/Alouette' Squadron at Bagotville.

Below: A rare one. The 101067 was the only EF–101B in service and was operated by 414 ECM Squadron at North Bay. It was well-known as the 'Electric' Voodoo.

Opposite: A colourful formation: CF–101B Voodoos of 409, 416, 425 and 414 Squadron flew during the farewell flight in the summer of 1984 over North Bay.

GERMANY

Below: July 22, 1983. On Lechfeld airbase JBG–32 celebrated its 25th anniversary. F104G 20+62 was brightened with a coloured tail and ditto tiptanks.

Opposite: The 25th jubilee of JBG–31 'Boelcke' on Norvenich A/B on April 30, 1983 coincided with the departure of the Starfighter. TF–104G 28+31 ended an era with dignity. The white sword of the squadron badge on a light blue background can be seen all over the fuselage. Note the front pilot, who wears the World War I helmet of 'der Kaiser'.

Below: F104G Starfighter N–104RB is the former DA+05 and 24+81. In 1982 this plane was painted in the colours of the Red Baron and became the gate-guard of Norvenich.

Opposite: On April 18, 1984 JBG–32 of Lechfeld again hit the news; their F104Gs were placed on the retired list. The photograph shows the farewell flight of the 20+36 in its special beautiful colour scheme.

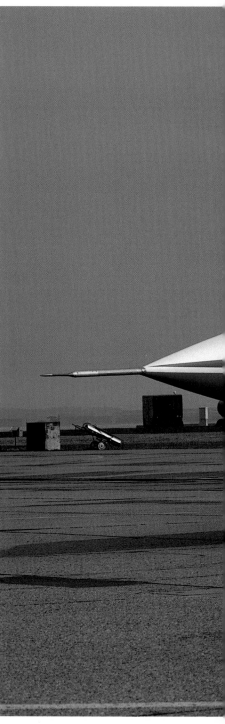

Below & Opposite: Over the years RF–4E Phantom 35+75 of AG–51 has proved to be very photogenic. During the TAM in 1978 it had flamboyant tiptanks and during the TAM in 1982 it wore AG–51 texts. The 25th jubilee of AG–51 on July 6, 1984 was the culmination. Though mostly white, both tail and wingtips were painted in the colours of GFR–Land Bavaria on the left, and in those of Baden-Württemberg on the right.

Overleaf: The best was not good enough in 1984. Together with AG–51, JBG–35 had existed for 25 years on July 6. Meanwhile, following tradition, this F–4F Phantom with serial 38+58 shows its wonderful colours.

Opposite: The serial of this F104G is a fiction: it is really 24+19. On May 5, 1984 this machine symbolised by means of the fake serial the 25 years of JBG–34 and 50 years of Flugplatz Memmingen.

Below: Twenty-five-year-old JG–71 'Richthofen' (Wittmund airbase) presented on April 28, 1984, this attractive F–4F Phantom 38+47.

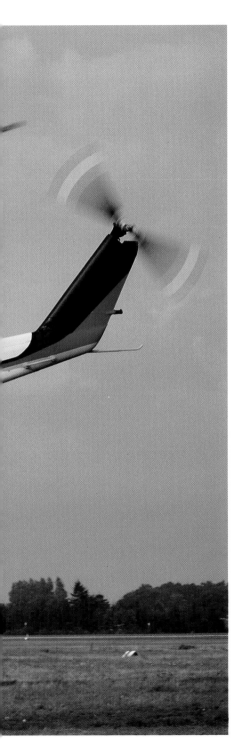

Opposite: Twenty-five years of HTG–64 (Ahlhorn A/B) at the same time meant 25 years of SAR (Search and Rescue) Flight. On September 22, 1984, the festivities were illuminated with a great SAR meeting. UH–1D 70+54 was the high point.

Below: It was a very rainy day when JBG–41 of Husum A/B celebrated its 25th jubilee on September 30, 1984. Alpha Jet 40+62 was flown before the public, but the bad weather spoiled a lot of the colours.

Below: Alpha Jet Operator JBG–43 of Oldenburg celebrated 25 years on November 11, 1984. Alpha Jet 40+44 concluded this year with beautiful colours.

Opposite: In June 1986 the World Helicopter Championship was held at Castle Ashby Estate in England. Qua colours somewhat adjusted, the Bölkow Bo–105 with serial 80+13 was one of the participants.

Opposite: The face of this Fiat G–91R 32+37 is painted for an open house of LVR–7 at Husum in 1986. During a night operation the G–91 is rolled into the barracks by a truck.

Below: On May 30, 1985 JBG–33 of Buchel A/B said farewell to the F–104G Starfighter. The serial, 21+67, is painted on the nosewheel doors.

Below & Opposite: Again a Starfighter — on September 12, we see 20+37 of LVR–1 in natural metal with white wings. These were the standard colours before camouflage entered the scene. The tail carried a badge with the emblems of all units that ever flew the F–104G.

Below: In September 1986 MFG–2 dismissed the Starfighter from duty, thus ending the era of this type with the Bundesmarine. The demo team, the 'Vikings', marked the retirement by painting its two machines, 26+63 and 26+72, in a festive way. On September 10 they were presented to the press on Eggebeck.

Opposite: This 'Blue Angel look-alike' F–4F Phantom 37+56 shows beyond doubt the reason for the festivities of September 27, 1986 on Neuburg A/B: the 25th anniversary of JG–74.

Opposite: In December 1986 again a 25th anniversary. This time LTG–63 of Hohn A/B. Though little publicity was given, Transall 51+02 was painted in a pretty colour.

Below: On September 14, JBG–36 of Rheine Hopsten celebrated its 25th anniversary and 'set aflame' F–4F Phantom 37+55. The serial was reduced to a very small one on the front nosewheel door.

Below: On June 28, 1987 Neuhausen A/B celebrated its 20th anniversary. This occasion did not pass by unmarked, as is shown by UH–1D 72+26 of Neuhausen-based HFS–10.

Opposite: When HFR–35 of Niedermendig celebrated 30 years on May 24, 1987 and held an open day, CH–53G 84+05 was the main attraction.

Below: F–104G Starfighter 20+49 painted to mark the 25th anniversary on July 9, 1987 of Luftwaffeschleuse 11, a maintenance and overhaul unit at Manching.

Opposite: On October 27, 1987, JBG–34 of Memmingen as the last Starfighter-Geschwader said farewell to this type. One-o-four' 22+55 showed the squadron badge, a brilliant landscape, in its tail while the serial was placed on the nosewheel doors.

Opposite: On September 20, 1987 it was LTG–61's turn. This Landsberg-based unit celebrated its 30 years and two aircraft were adorned with a special scheme. The first one was Transall 50+96. It was not for the first time, because in these very colours the same machine made its debut during the public day at Ramstein on August 2.

Below: The second machine, Bell UH–1D 71+56, also flew with LTG–61 and its colour scheme had a lot in common with that of the Transall.

Below & Opposite: On August 28, 1988, JBG–31 of Norvenich painted her sword on Tornado 44+00, thus celebrating its 30 years' existence. Five years earlier it had appeared on the Starfighter (below).

Below: Another machine shown during the retreat of the F–104G at Memmingen was 24+19. An old acquaintance, seen before at Memmingen on May 5, 1984, at that time bearing the fake serial 25+50.

Opposite: JBG–32 of Lechfeld, also commemorated its 30 years' jubilee: on September 11, 1988, showing off Tornado 44+50.

Opposite: In September 1989, at Beja A/B in Portugal, this unidentified F–104G Starfighter could be admired. Again a withdrawal was the reason and true to tradition 'they did something about it'.

Below: The last Luftwaffe unit to withdraw the F–104G Starfighter: LVR–1 of Erding. 22+91 ended an era on March 20, 1989.

UNITED KINGDOM

Below: Phantom FGR–2 XV–486 and XV–424 of 56 Squadron wearing a special paint scheme to mark the 60th anniversary of the epic flight of Alcock and Brown. XV–424 crossed the Atlantic on June 21, 1979 from Goose Bay to Greenham Common, thus honouring Alcock and Brown's crossing 60 years earlier.

Opposite: In 1983 the biannual Air Tattoo at Greenham Common was dominated by the 25th anniversary of the F–4 Phantom. Already far from being dull this Phantom FGR–2 XT–597 of A&AEE Boscombe Down was labelled with several texts. Clearly one can see in which countries this type is in service . . .

Opposite: In 1986 and 1987 Hawks T–1 XX–172 and XX–238 made demo flights all over Europe, flying the Union Jack on their tails. Later on the paintings were revised a little. The purpose was the promotion of this BAe product. It was not in vain, as was proved by an order from Switzerland.

Below & Opposite: Number 2 Squadron of Laarbruch had been in existence for 60 years in 1988. Jaguar GR–1 XZ–104 with a black tail and a large emblem.

1912   ▲⬤▲   1988

II A.C. SQUADRON II
ROYAL AIR FORCE
HEREWARD

XZ1

Opposite: On May 1, 1989, Chinook HC-1 ZA-671 had a tail painting to mark the 75th anniversary of 7 Squadron at Odiham.

Below: In 1989, 9 Squadron at Bruggen celebrated its 75 years of existence. Furnished with a rather simple painting, Tornado GR.1 visited many shows. Here we see the machine at Wattisham on June 24, 1989.

FRANCE

Below: Bearing the escadre colours on its tail, Mirage 3E 3–JH of EC2/3 'Champagne' symbolises 35 years' *acte de presence* of the 3 Escadre de Chasse, which was founded in May 1950. This photo was taken in July 1985 at Bierset.

Opposite: With this artistic looking escadre badge 'a Hache' (battle axe) Mirage 3R, 317 of ER1/33 'Belfort' showed off over Strasbourg-Entzheim on June 26, 1986.

Below: One of the most famous squadrons of
the French Airforce is undoubtedly EC2/4 'La
Fayette'. Founded during World War I, it
celebrated its 70th birthday on October 4,
1986 with an airshow at Luxeuil. Two Mirages
3E, 4–BJ (619) and 4–BI (568) were shown in
appropriate colours.

Opposite: A Mirage F–1C with serial 5–NL
(205) of EC1/5 in a '50,000 hours' scheme at
Orange A/B on June 12, 1987. The name of Gal
Guegen, just below the cockpit, is that of the
commanding general of the CAFDA of
Defence Aerienne. It was this general who
actually flew the 50,000th hour on the F–1C.

Below & Opposite: On May 31, 1987, 13 Escadre de Chasse celebrated its 30th anniversary with a great airshow at Colmar. The three units based at this A/B each showed a Mirage in their own jubilee colours. These were: Mirage 3E of EC1/13 'Artois', Mirage 5F of EC2/13 'Folie', and Mirage 5F of EC3/13 'Morietur'. As usual, the serials are missing.

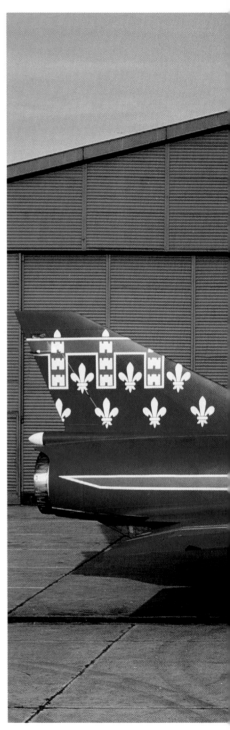

Below: November 1987, 61 Escadre de Transport at Orléans-Bricy was the first unit to get it all at once. For twenty years it flew the C–160 Transall and at the same time flew its 500,000th hour . . . reason enough for this Transall to show some pretty colours. The emblem on its tail is that of COTAM and shows two ducks towing a turtle.

Opposite: ERV–94 at Istres received the last of eleven C–135FRs with serial CI (12737) on April 13, 1988. Boeing converted these machines and equipped them with new CFM turbofans. The transfer was celebrated by eye-catching ceremonial.

Below & Opposite: The departure of the Mirage 3RD of ER3/33 at Strasbourg: 33–TG (358) was painted in special colours. On June 19, 1988 it was flown before the public. While one side showed the text '33eme Escadre de Reconnaissance', the opposite side made clear that the unit had flown 90,000 hours.

Bottom: Commemoration of the retirement of the Jaguar with EC4/7 at Istres-Le Tube on August 1, 1989: A64/7–NE and A67/7–NB painted with the French Tricolor. The badges of both escadrilles ('Aigle' and 'Fennec') were painted on both left and right sides of the tail.

Below: At Le Luc A/B these two TB–30 Epsilons were shown on June 26, 1989 telling that this type flew 100,000 hours. Three planes, under which the 315–VV (49) and 315–WA (56) looked almost like civil aircraft.

Opposite: This time not a jubilee of the French Airforce but 200 years of France's Great Revolution. At Colmar on May 21, 1989 this Mirage IIIB with serial 245 of EC1/13 is shown in Bicentennial colours during the open day.

ITALY

Below: Fiat G–91Y 8–04 of the 8th Stormo at Cervia-San Giorgio (Italy) painted in December 1983 with a Christmas outfit, and visited all AMI bases.

Opposite: Trevisi-San Angeloa A/B on May 17, 1987. Two notable events were celebrated. The 2nd Stormo existed 30 years and had flown 200,000 hours with the Fiat G–91R. Reason enough to paint 2–34 (MM.6244) in a beautiful outfit.

Below & Opposite: A serial number will not be found on this F–104G, but believe it or not this is the 37–20. This colour scheme was worn during the 50th anniversary celebrations of 37 Stormo at Trapani Birgi on April 1, 1989.

Below: As a countermeasure after the blotting of a Dutch F–16B during a rotation at Gioia del Colle (Italy), the dress of this F–104S (MM.6850) of 12° Gruppo at A/B Twenthe on June 16, 1989 was adjusted a bit . . .

Opposite: Based at Rimini, F–104ASA 5–11 (MM.6833) was the high point of the RNeth. A/F open day at Volkel on September 29, 1989. With this machine 102° Gruppo commemorated its 25 years of flying the Starfighter.

Below: At AMI's A/B Grosseto this F–104S 4–27 (MM.6546) of 5° Stormo was painted 'Ferrari red' so as to publicize the Ferrari Club on September 19, 1989.

Left & Below: For the first meet of 28° Gruppo, November 1989 at Villafranca, this RF–104G 'Strega Fighter' 3–42 (MM.6579) was painted in really superb squadron colours.

THE NETHERLANDS

Opposite: December 1982: F–104G (D–8337) passes 3,000 flying hours and is unofficially scribbled on. The text, 'Still the best there is', had an ironic sound when this aircraft was the next Klu Starfighter to crash on April 12, 1983 in England.

Right & Below: On June 10, 1983, 322 Squadron at Leeuwarden celebrated 40 years and F–16A J–252's tail was coloured. With this colour still on its tail, the machine crashed after a bird-hit during take-off at Leeuwarden on October 4, 1983.

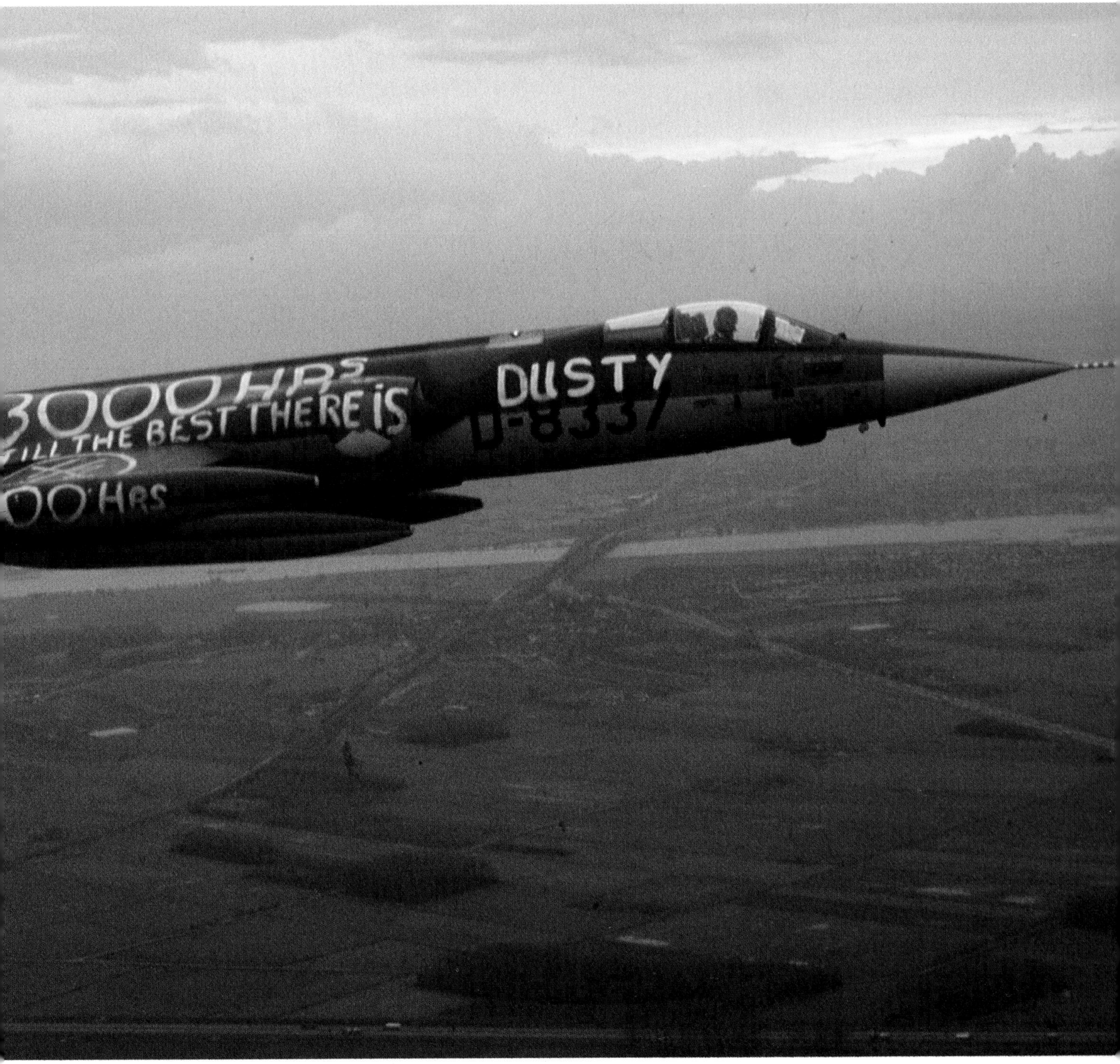
3000 HRS
TILL THE BEST THERE IS
DUSTY
D-8337
00 HRS

Below: To celebrate its 35th anniversary on May 7, 1986, 311 Squadron poked fun at this F–16A J–616.

Opposite: On the yearly visitors' day of the Koninklijke Luchtmacht, held on September 20, 1986 at Eindhoven, the J–616 of 311 Squadron was still flown as demo. The text, 'Open day KLU 86', was added.

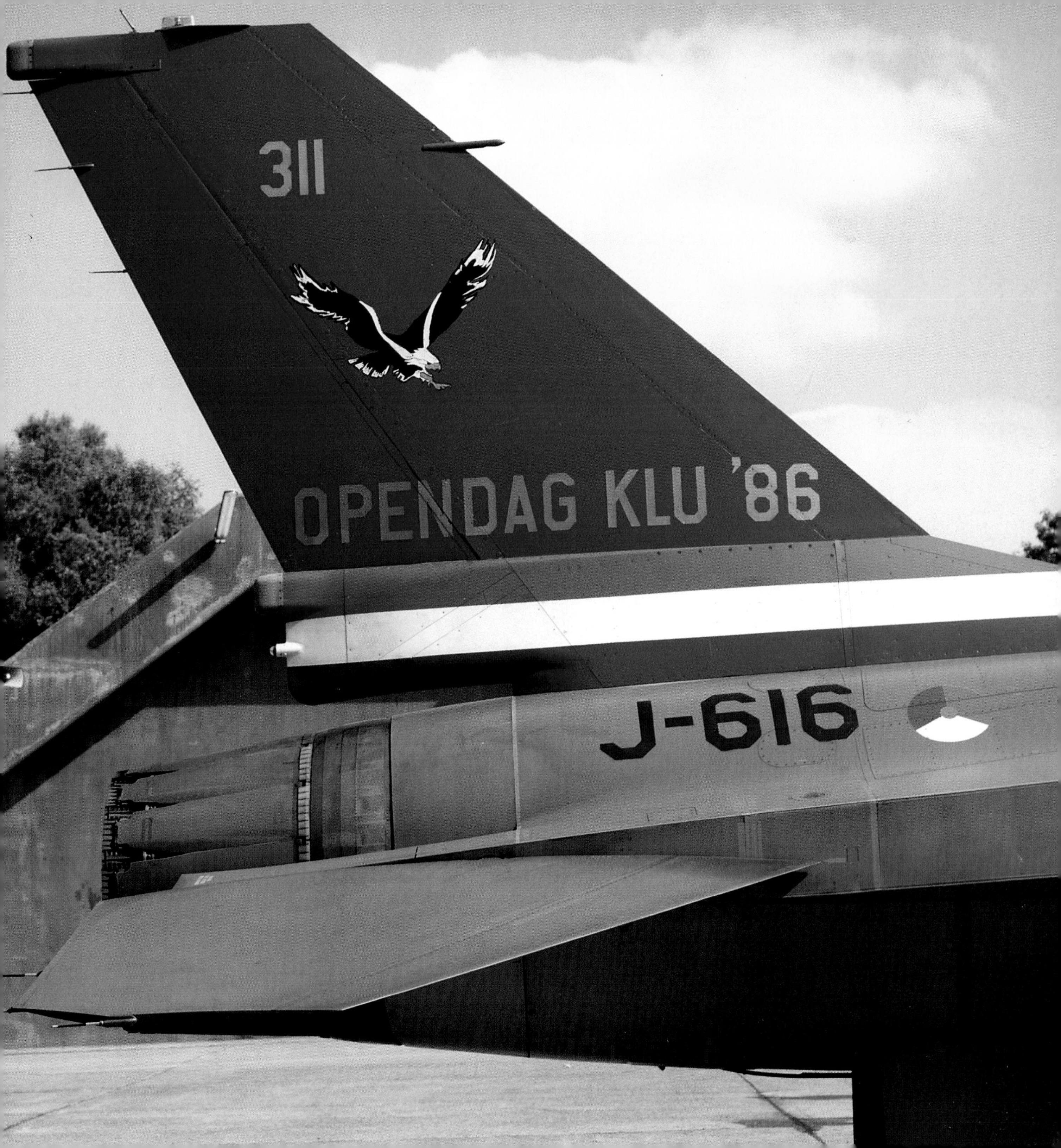
311
OPENDAG KLU '86
J-616

Below & Opposite: In 1988 the Koninklijke Luchtmacht was 75 years old. 314 Squadron formed an occasional team with two NF–5s. For this team, named 'Synchro-pair display Double Dutch', no less than five NF–5s were painted in display colours, first in a very rigid scheme of lines but later on interrupted by the 'Double Dutch' badge on the nose. In turn the team used the K–3012, K–3014, K–3042, K–3054 and K–3072.

Below: The F–16A display of 1988 was fulfilled by 312 Squadron. 'KLu–75' also dominated the colours of this J–864.

Opposite: The demo team of 334 Squadron, famous because of their airshows with the Fokker F–27, in 1988 painted their machine, the C–5, in a 'KLu–75' outfit.

Below & Opposite: On July 1, 1988, 313 Squadron said farewell to the NF–5 and symbolised this with the K–3045. On the tail the squadron wrote its parting words: at the right it expressed its thanks and at the left hinted at the fact that the Netherlands football team had recently won the European Cup.

Below: On June 7, 1989 it was ten years since the J–259 was delivered as the very first F–16(B) to the Royal Netherlands A/F. Decorated with the national tricolor with the Frisian flag on top of the tail, this aircraft visited all Netherlands A/F bases that day.

Opposite: Military vandalism or just a friendly happening? This picture was taken when F–16B, J–210 returned from a rotation at Gioia del Colle in Italy on June 15, 1989. The mascot, the horse of 12 Gruppo, 'got over it'. So, it was friendly after all!

NF–5 SOLO-DISPLAY TEAM

Apart from a few aircraft having coloured tails, the Royal Netherlands Air Force never made a fuss of squadron jubilees. Quite different was the situation with the NF–5 Solo-Display Team, which impressed everyone over a number of years. However, far from being a real demo team like the Red Arrows, it was more like an occasional team rotating amongst the various NF–5 squadrons. Nevertheless, it eventually lasted for more than eight years. This special status makes it deserve a place in this book.

The rotating system meant that every two years a different squadron, with its own pilots and different machines, flying revised colours, provided the team. Finally, when each NF–5 squadron had taken the team under its wings for two years, the enthusiasm to continue was reduced to zero. Therefore in 1984 the displays were ended and in 1985 the team was officially abolished.

Below: The third phase of the display team fell in 1981/82 when 315 Squadron took over the K–3019 and K–3024.

Opposite: The start of the display team, with only two machines, NF–5A K–3031 and K–3048 of 316 Squadron during display celebrating 65 years of Royal Netherlands A/F in 1978.

Below: The final stage. In 1983/84, 314 Squadron took the display team under its wings and flew in turn with K–3021 and K–3026.

Opposite: In 1979/80 the demo flights were furnished by 313 Squadron with K–3028 and K–3041.

UNITED STATES (USAFE)

Opposite: 316 Air Division is the master organisation of 86 TFW. Its commander's machine, F–16C 84.1316, furnished with a large emblem on its tail, also on June 25, 1986 at Ramstein.

Below: On June 25, 1986 the commander's machine of 86 TFW, an F–16C with serial 84.1286 RS, wearing a red and white tail, was pictured at Ramstein. At the same time it wore the badges of 512 TFS, 526 TFS and 417 TFS.

SWEDEN

Below: Probably to promote an air show in 1990, this J–35F Draken (35468) of 1 Jaktflygdivisionen of Flygflottiljen F'10 of Angelholm A/B was photographed on August 19, 1989 at Halmstad.

Opposite: As a replacement for the F–35F Draken, Flottilj F–16 of Uppsala A/B in February 1986 received their first JA–37 Viggen. Draken 35475/11 was dressed up in a farewell style.

SWITZERLAND

Opposite: To celebrate 75 years of Switzerland's Airforce on January 15, 1989, this Hunter F–58 J–4007 of Fliegerstaffel 7 at Payerne was dressed up in an eye-catching manner.

NATO TIGERMEET

The NATO Tigermeet is a remarkable event and because of the attractive 'tiger-like' decorated aircraft it is an inevitable part of the 'Colourful Eighties', and of the preceding period. In 1990 the Tiger organisation had existed for thirty years — which makes it necessary to depict its history in brief.

Since its foundation in 1961 the Tiger organisation has each year organised a great reunion/fly-in meet. It is an international happening, borders are no dividing-line and the reunion has been held in several countries. Participants in principle can be all NATO airforces, provided they delegate a unit that flies a tiger as symbol. It is this tiger which explains the name — and this principle is honoured very strictly indeed.

The exception proves the rule — also in the Tigermeet! The exception is the (West) German Staffel 431, part of Jagdbombergeschwader 43 and based at Oldenburg A/B. Being equipped with the Alpha Jet, this unit in fact has a fox's head as emblem. In order to take part in the Tiger organisation, the text 'Believe it or not, this is a tiger' was added. The squadron was accepted as a member and ever since the 'tiger fox' (or is it 'fox tiger'?) has given rise to much hilarity during the reunion.

Yet another intruder is 230 Squadron of the Royal Air Force. Equipped with Puma helicopters, this squadron takes a notable place within a reunion that is dominated by fighter squadrons. Together with the Portuguese 301 Squadron, this 'heli' unit only became a member of the Tiger organisation in 1978. One year before it had fulfilled many tasks during a reunion/fly-in at Greenham Common in England.

The Tigermeet meanwhile has survived many occasions of international tension, such as financial crises and even coups d'état. The international 'tiger spirit' was not weakened — on the contrary, the number of participants kept growing. Thus Switzerland joined the Tiger guild and takes a remarkable place as a non-aligned country.

A good feature of the Tiger organisation is the combination of the reunion/fly-in with an airshow for the public. Traditionally the home team paints one of its airplanes in full Tiger colours. Over the years, many strange 'tigers' have flown over Europe. The airplanes are depicted in this special Tiger chapter. But first an historic outline.

ORIGIN AND GOAL OF THE TIGERMEET

What is so special about the Tigermeet and what is its aim? Having survived for about thirty years and still growing, it must be an extraordinary meet, so let's give it a closer look.

The first Tigermeet was held in 1961 at RAF Woodford. The idea for this meet arose when the then French Minister of War made a plea to intensify French-American relations.

From this French plea, USAF's 79 TFS, then based at Woodford, England, worked out the idea to found a league of fighter squadrons all flying a tiger as squadron emblem. The Escadron de Chasse 1/12 of Cambrai (France) was invited to Woodford, together with 74 RAF Squadron. The first Tigermeet took place.

The meet was a great success and during the second meet one year later, also held at Woodford, no fewer than eight squadrons from six countries gathered. From that time stems the decision of the Tiger organisation to make it a yearly event and to grant each year another squadron the role of host squadron.

The main purpose of the meet is to make and maintain social contacts in order to establish a good mutual understanding between the partners. This led to a series of flying exercises and competitions of professional quality. General Robert M. Lee put his seal upon the event by introducing in January 1966 the Air Deputy Award. This award should keep the idea behind the Tigermeet alive. Partly because of lack of financial funds from the official side, the Tiger organisation threatened to bleed to death at the beginning of the eighties. The low point was reached with the reunion of 1982 when at Gütersloh A/B in Germany only the very minimum of participants showed up. In 1983 the Tigermeet was held at the Canadian base Baden Söllingen in the GFR. 439 Squadron acted as host and introduced a renewed programme. Part of the rejuvenation was the element of competition and also the tightening up of the mutual ties. This gave the Tigermeet a new lease of life.

THE FUTURE

Today, with three decades of Tigermeet behind us, the Tigermeet again faces a new low point. A number of fatal accidents, especially in the GFR, gave rise to great public and political pressure to end all air shows. A direct consequence of this pressure was the cancellation of the 29th Tigermeet in 1989, planned at Oldenburg A/B in (West) Germany. A sad comedown — for the first time in its existence the Tigermeet had to be cancelled. For this reason the future of the event is very uncertain indeed. On the other hand, bearing in mind that the détente between East and West is moulding into concrete forms, the Tigermeet might become a truly international event. Freedom, equality and fraternity — these words could be the motto of a revived Tigermeet. Who could oppose this, especially at this turning-point in history?

Opposite: As a 'take-off run' to the eighties, a Dassault Mystère B-2 of the French EC 1/12 during the seventeenth Tigermeet at Greenham Common in 1977.

Below: FX–52, a Belgian F–104G Starfighter of 31 Smaldeel, at its home base, Kleine Brogel, in 1978.

Pilot
Capt "Jake" Mentz

U.S. AIR FO
AF SERIAL
SERVICE TH
GRADE JP-
PER ASTM

AMBIENT SENSING PORT
CABIN PRESSURE REGULATOR
DO NOT PLUG OR
DEFORM HOLES
KEEP SMOOTH AND
CLEAR WITHIN CIRCLE

STEP
RELEASE TOWN SLOP
CLOSE/ALIGN
MARKS

247

FB-III A
MAX WEIGHT 114,900 lbs
WING SPAN-SWEPT-34'
MAX SPEED-HIGH
HEIGHT 17
WING

Below: During the 20th Tigermeet at Cameri (Italy) in 1980, the host failed to show up. The Canadian 439 Squadron retrieved the situation with CF–104G 104439.

Opposite: Mirage F–1 12–YE of host squadron EC 1/12 was painted with a tiger tail during the meet at Cambrai in 1979.

Opposite: The Canadians had come to like it and 439 Squadron was notably present at Bitburg with CF–104G 104761.

Below: Of course 439 Squadron at Söllingen showed up with its own aircraft — this time Starfighter 104706.

Below: An intruder, though in tiger colours, was Puma HC–1 of 230 RAF Squadron at Gütersloh in 1982.

Opposite: Though the 22nd Tigermeet at Gütersloh was a low point, these two tiger whelps were not to blame.

Opposite, Below & Overleaf: In 1984 the Tigermeet was held at Leck (GFR) and Aufklärungs-Geschwader 52 was true to tradition with this 35+76, a McDonnell-Douglas RF–4E Phantom. At the left on its tail it flew the Geschwader-badge and on the right the one of the Staffel.

Below: In 1985 the 25th anniversary was celebrated at Kleine Brogel in Belgium. FA–62, a F–16A of 31 Smaldeel, was disguised as a tiger but had to make a clean breast of it after a short flight. In large placards the machine lost its tiger skin.

Below & Opposite: In 1986 we find the meeting at Cambrai (France) again. This time not an adapted F–1 of the host but two Super Etendarts of Aéronautique Navale's 11 Flotille. Both machines, number 7 and number 35, showed with some variation a tiger coming out of the intake. Well, according to their tails they looked more like spider-monkeys!

Overleaf: For many years 301 Escuadron of the Portuguese Airforce tried to get the Tigermeet to Montijo in Portugal. In 1987 they succeeded and Fiat G–91R 5465 was dressed up in a superb way.

POUR LIBÉRER LE PILOTE
BRISER LA GLACE
ET EN S'ÉCARTANT TIRER L'ANNEAU

Below: As if to say that the Fiat was not enough the 'Museu do Ar' painted one of her still flying T–6 Harvards (1774) partly in tiger colours.

Opposite: In 1988 the Tigermeet was held at Cameri in Italy for the third time. Enough reason for 21 Gruppo to outfit F–104S Starfighter 53–06/MM.6825 beautifully.

Below: Outside and in addition, a Fiat G–91R
of the German Leichtenkampf-Geschwader 43
on a public day at Oldenburg in 1984. The
machine, 31+00, is displayed here as a
memorial to days long past when LKG–43 flew
this type.